50 free original recipes

welcome to
50 free
original recipes

If you love meaty main courses and delicious fish dishes, this recipe book is about to become your best friend!

50 Free Original Recipes features a delicious collection of hunger-busting meal ideas that you and your family will love. Focusing on everyday ingredients, it's packed with inspiration for every occasion, from simple light bites to elegant entertaining, and everything in between!

As well as being super-simple to create, every single recipe is Free on our Original and Extra Easy choices – so they're perfect for your weight loss too.

- Enjoy a finger-licking feast with masala crab cakes, aromatic seekh kebabs and warming ginger chicken wings.

- Tuck into family favourites like luxury fish pie, beefed-up burgers and sweet and sour chicken.

- Our Mexican-style prawn and pepper stir-fry, aromatic lamb tagine and Thai pork curry will really spice things up.

- Make the perfect Sunday dinner… whatever the day with turkey with pesto and roasted veg or mustard and garlic-roasted leg of lamb – delicious!

Split into six chapters, with tempting photography throughout, **50 Free Original Recipes** is yet another way to help you enjoy every bite on the journey to weight loss success.

contents

soups and starters

Perfect for a light bite or as a starter
to a Food Optimising feast, you'll find
inspiration galore right here…

cock-a-leekie soup

serves 4

each serving is:

Free on Original

Free on Extra Easy

freezer friendly

ready in 40 minutes

500g skinless and boneless chicken breasts, cut into bite-sized pieces

2 onions, peeled and finely chopped

2 carrots, peeled and sliced

1 litre chicken stock

500g leeks, trimmed and thinly sliced

a large handful of fresh flat-leaf parsley

salt and freshly ground black pepper

Cock-a-leekie is a classic Scottish soup using leeks and chicken stock. This soup dates back to the 16th century and traditionally included prunes for sweetness – this version takes sweetness from the carrots.

Place the chicken, onions, carrots and stock into a heavy-based pan and bring to the boil. Add the leeks and parsley and bring back to the boil. Reduce the heat to low and cook gently for 25-30 minutes or until the leeks are tender, and the chicken is cooked.

Remove from the heat and season well before serving.

For extra flavour replace the parsley with a bouquet garni. You can buy ready-made ones but for really special depth of flavour make your own by bundling up 1 bay leaf, 4 sprigs of parsley (flat-leaf or curly), 3 sprigs of fresh thyme, a 10cm piece celery and a 10cm piece of the green part of a leek, and tying them together with string. Remove before serving.

hungarian goulash soup

serves 4

each serving is:

Free on Original

Free on Extra Easy

freezer friendly

ready in 45-50 minutes

1 green pepper, deseeded and chopped

2 carrots, peeled and diced

1 large onion, peeled and chopped

1-2 garlic cloves, peeled and crushed

1.1 litres beef stock

225g lean rump steak, all visible fat removed, diced

1 tbsp paprika

½ tsp caraway seeds

4 tomatoes

1 level tbsp tomato purée

salt and freshly ground black pepper

fat free natural yogurt and chopped fresh flat-leaf parsley, to serve

Hearty, substantial comfort food, this is a soup that makes you look forward to winter! Paprika is the key ingredient to any good goulash – reduce or increase the amount depending on how much heat you want.

Place the vegetables in a large heavy-based saucepan with 275ml of the stock, cover and bring to the boil.

Boil for 5-10 minutes then add the diced steak, paprika, caraway seeds and the remaining stock. Stir well and simmer gently for 15 minutes.

Meanwhile prick the tomatoes, place in a bowl of boiling water for 2 minutes, then drain and remove the skin. Chop the tomatoes and add to the pan with the tomato purée. Season well and continue simmering for another 15 minutes, until the steak and vegetables are cooked and tender.

Serve the soup topped with a swirl of yogurt and some chopped parsley.

For a really distinctive smoky flavour use smoked paprika rather than standard paprika.

thai prawn and lemon grass soup

serves 4

each serving is:

Free on Original

Free on Extra Easy

freezer friendly

ready in about 10 minutes

Fragrant, warm and comforting, this light, flavoursome soup is perfect for a cold evening. This recipe would also work really well with cooked shredded chicken instead of the prawns, or even a mixture of the two. Ready in 10 minutes, you'll soon be warmed up *and* full up!

6 spring onions, trimmed and finely shredded

2 lemon grass stalks, very finely sliced

1 garlic clove, peeled and crushed

5mm piece root ginger, peeled and finely grated

1 red chilli, deseeded and finely sliced (optional)

850ml chicken stock

60g shiitake mushrooms, thinly sliced

60g mangetout, thinly sliced

200g raw tiger prawns, peeled

1 tbsp dark soy sauce

2 tbsp chopped fresh coriander

Place the spring onions, lemon grass, garlic, ginger, red chilli and stock in a large saucepan, cover and bring to the boil.

Add the mushrooms and mangetout and cook briskly for 3-4 minutes, then add the prawns and soy sauce. Cook for a further 2-3 minutes until the prawns turn pink. Remove from the heat.

Stir in the chopped coriander and serve immediately.

For the freshest, tastiest lemon grass look out for stalks that are firm, not soft and rubbery which means it's too old. The lower stalk should be pale yellow, almost white, while the upper stalks should be green, not brown.

ginger chicken wings

Fresh root ginger is widely used in Indian cuisine to impart a rich flavour to many vegetable, meat and poultry dishes. In this recipe it's used to add extra zing to chicken wings – with great results!

Place the chicken wings in a large mixing bowl. Mix together the ginger, sea salt, Tabasco, garlic, lemon juice, sweetener and yogurt and pour over the chicken. Toss well to combine, cover and marinate in the fridge overnight.

When ready to cook, remove the wings from the marinade, place on a grill rack, lightly spray with low calorie cooking spray and sprinkle with the chilli powder and black pepper.

Cook under a medium grill for 10-12 minutes, turning once or twice or until the wings are cooked through and lightly browned. Serve immediately on a bed of mixed salad leaves with limes wedges to squeeze over.

serves 4

each serving is:

Free on Original

Free on Extra Easy

freezer friendly

ready in 20 minutes
plus overnight marinating

12 large skinless
chicken wings

2cm piece root ginger,
peeled and finely grated

2 tsp sea salt

2 tsp Tabasco sauce

2 garlic cloves,
peeled and crushed

juice of 2 lemons

½ tsp sweetener

4 tbsp fat free natural yogurt

low calorie cooking spray

½ tsp mild chilli powder

½ tsp freshly ground
black pepper

mixed salad leaves, to serve

lime wedges, to garnish

chicken liver pâté

This pâté is smooth and velvety and makes a stunning starter for a dinner party. Serving it with salad helps to cut through the richness of the liver.

serves 4

each serving is:

Free on Original

Free on Extra Easy

freezer friendly

ready in about 25 minutes plus overnight chilling

low calorie cooking spray

500g chicken livers, trimmed and cleaned

4 lean bacon rashers, all visible fat removed, very finely chopped

1 onion, peeled and finely chopped

3 garlic cloves, peeled and finely chopped

2 tsp chopped fresh thyme leaves

¼ tsp English mustard powder

2 tsp finely crushed black peppercorns

2 tsp sea salt

300g quark

Spray a large non-stick frying pan with low calorie cooking spray and place over a high heat. Add the livers and bacon and fry quickly on all sides until golden, but still pink in the middle, about 6-8 minutes. Place the livers, bacon and pan juices in a food processor.

Spray the same pan again with low calorie cooking spray and place over a medium heat. Add the onion and garlic, and cook over a moderate heat until the onion is soft but not coloured. Add the thyme, mustard, black pepper and sea salt, and scrape the bottom of the pan to release any juices.

Add the onion mixture to the food processor together with the quark and blend until smooth.

Divide the mixture between four individual ramekins, smooth the tops and chill for 24 hours before serving.

Serve this pâté with vegetable batons, or spread onto crisp little gem lettuce leaves.

seekh
kebabs

These aromatic spiced minced beef kebabs are often cooked on open braziers or grills in small roadside restaurants throughout northern India. Here they're baked to perfection and make a great starter.

serves 4
each serving is:
Free on Original
Free on Extra Easy

freezer friendly
ready in 35 minutes
plus overnight marinating

Place all the ingredients, except the low calorie cooking spray, in a mixing bowl and use your fingers to combine thoroughly. Cover and marinate in the fridge overnight to allow the flavours to develop.

Preheat the oven to 190°C/Gas 5 and line a baking sheet with baking parchment. Divide the meat mixture into 12 portions and shape each one around a metal or bamboo skewer to make a sausage shape about 10cm in length.

Place the kebabs on the prepared baking sheet and lightly spray with low calorie cooking spray. Bake for 15-20 minutes, turning them once halfway through cooking. Remove from the oven and serve with some fat free natural yogurt sprinkled with chilli powder and salad of your choice.

1 fresh green chilli, deseeded and finely chopped

2 tsp ground ginger

5 garlic cloves, peeled and crushed

2 tbsp finely chopped fresh coriander

1 tsp roasted cumin seeds

500g extra lean minced beef

2 tbsp peeled and finely chopped red onion

1 tsp mild or medium chilli powder

1 small egg, beaten

2 tsp sea salt

low calorie cooking spray

fat free natural yogurt and salad, to serve

ham and
egg soufflés

A step up from a ham omelette, these individual soufflés also make a lovely light lunch served with a crisp green salad.

serves 4

each serving is:

Free on Original

Free on Extra Easy

ready in 22-25 minutes

low calorie cooking spray

2 large eggs, separated

110g lean ham,
all visible fat removed,
finely chopped

1 tbsp finely chopped
fresh tarragon

4 tbsp finely chopped
fresh flat-leaf parsley

1 tbsp finely chopped
fresh chives

salt and freshly ground
black pepper

Preheat the oven to 200°C/Gas 6. Lightly spray four individual ovenproof soufflé dishes with low calorie cooking spray and place on a baking sheet.

In a bowl beat the egg yolks until pale and fluffy. Stir in the chopped ham and herbs and season well.

Whisk the egg whites in a separate bowl until softly peaked and, using a metal spoon, fold into the ham mixture. Spoon this mixture into the prepared dishes and bake for 12-15 minutes until risen and golden. Remove from the oven and serve immediately.

This soufflé is delicious with prawns rather than ham. Swap the tarragon for fresh dill.

smoked **trout** florentine
with dill hollandaise dressing

A simple dish of trout fillets served on a bed of spinach and drizzled with a hollandaise-style dressing. Salmon or mackerel would make good alternatives to the trout.

serves 4

each serving is:

Free on Original

Free on Extra Easy

ready in 15 minutes

Make the hollandaise dressing by placing all the ingredients, except the seasoning, into a blender and process until smooth. Season to taste, transfer to a bowl and set aside.

Spray a large non-stick frying pan with low calorie cooking spray. Place over a medium heat and add the garlic and spinach. Stir and cook for 3-4 minutes or until the spinach has just wilted. Season well and remove from the heat.

To serve, divide the spinach mixture between four plates in neat mounds and top with the trout fillets. Spoon over the dressing and serve immediately.

for the dressing

4 tbsp quark

8 tbsp fat free natural fromage frais

60ml hot chicken stock

6 tbsp finely chopped dill

2 tbsp finely chopped chives

1 tsp English mustard powder

salt and freshly ground black pepper

for the trout

low calorie cooking spray

2 garlic cloves, peeled and finely chopped

400g baby leaf spinach

4 x 110g hot-smoked trout fillets

If you're not a spinach fan this dish would also work well with sliced beetroot.

smoked salmon terrine

serves 4

each serving is:

Free on Original

Free on Extra Easy

freezer friendly

ready in 25 minutes
plus chilling

This elegant and attractive starter will wow your guests. It makes for easy entertaining as you prepare it ahead and refrigerate until set.

450g thinly cut smoked salmon slices

15g powdered gelatine

200ml hot fish stock

2 garlic cloves, peeled and crushed

6 tbsp finely chopped fresh dill

200g quark

2 tbsp pink peppercorns

juice of 1 lemon

salt and freshly ground black pepper

fresh dill sprigs and lemon wedges, to garnish

Line a small 450g loaf tin with cling film. Using half of the smoked salmon slices, line the tin, ensuring you overlap the slices and the top slices overhang the sides of the tin.

Sprinkle the gelatine over the hot stock and stir to dissolve completely.

Roughly chop the remaining salmon and place in a food processor with the garlic, dill, quark, peppercorns and lemon juice. Pour in the gelatine liquid, season well and process until smooth. Spoon this mixture into the lined tin and enclose with the overhanging salmon slices. Cover and refrigerate overnight or for a minimum of 3 hours until set.

To serve, carefully turn out the terrine, peel away the cling film and cut into thick slices. Garnish with fresh dill and lemon wedges.

masala
crab cakes

These crab cakes originate from the southern coast of western India. Here they are mixed with firm white fish to give you a spicy, flavoursome cake that's a great starter or makes a terrific light lunch when served with a salad.

Place the crabmeat, white fish, curry powder, garlic, red chilli, red onion, coriander and egg in a food processor. Season and process for a few seconds until well mixed. Transfer to a mixing bowl and, using your fingers, mix well. Cover and chill in the fridge for 5-6 hours (or overnight if time permits) to allow the mixture to firm up and let the flavours combine.

Preheat the oven to 200°C/Gas 6. Line a baking sheet with non-stick baking parchment and spray with low calorie cooking spray. Divide the crab mixture into 12 portions and shape each one into a cake.

Place on the prepared baking sheet and bake for 20-25 minutes or until lightly browned and cooked through. Serve garnished with coriander, red pepper and lemon wedges, with the yogurt on the side to dip into.

If you can't find fresh crabmeat, use canned.

serves 4

each serving is:

Free on Original

Free on Extra Easy

freezer friendly

ready in 30 minutes
plus chilling

200g fresh white crabmeat

200g white fish fillet
(eg cod or halibut),
roughly chopped

1 tbsp mild curry powder

2 garlic cloves,
peeled and crushed

1 red chilli, deseeded
and finely chopped

4 tbsp peeled and finely
chopped red onion

4 tbsp chopped
fresh coriander

1 small egg, beaten

salt and freshly ground
black pepper

low calorie cooking spray

chopped fresh coriander,
finely chopped red pepper
and lemon wedges, to
garnish

fat free natural yogurt,
to serve

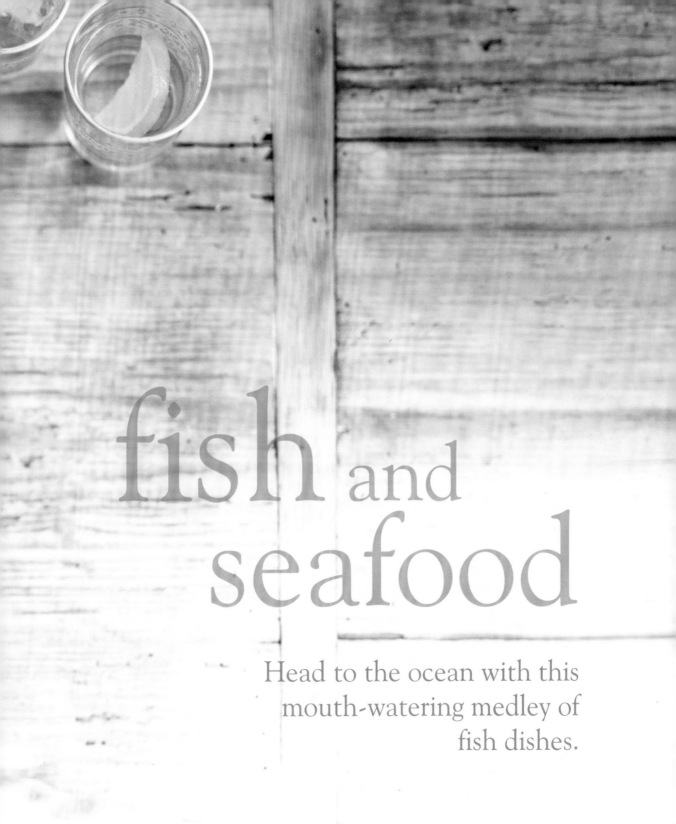

fish and seafood

Head to the ocean with this mouth-watering medley of fish dishes.

moroccan spiced
fish kebab salad

serves 4

each serving is:

Free on Original

Free on Extra Easy

ready in 20 minutes
plus marinating

150g fat free natural yogurt

1 garlic clove,
peeled and crushed

½ tsp ground coriander

2 tsp ground cumin

½ tsp ground cinnamon

1 tsp freshly ground
black pepper

1.5cm piece root ginger,
peeled and finely grated

500g monkfish fillets,
skinned

2 small red onions, peeled
and cut into wedges

8 baby plum or
cherry tomatoes

fresh mint leaves,
to garnish

lime wedges, to serve

Firm-textured monkfish is perfect for these succulent kebabs, although raw tiger or king prawns can be used instead. Allow time for marinating, so that the spices can infuse the fish with their warm flavours.

Place the yogurt, garlic, coriander, cumin, cinnamon, pepper and ginger in a bowl. Stir to mix well.

Wash the monkfish and pat dry with kitchen paper, then cut into bite-sized chunks. Add to the yogurt mixture, turning to coat completely. Cover and leave to marinate in the fridge for 2 hours.

Preheat the grill. Remove the fish from the marinade and thread on to 8 metal or pre-soaked bamboo skewers, alternating them with the onion wedges and tomatoes. Brush with the remaining marinade.

Place the kebabs on the grill rack and cook under the grill for about 10 minutes, turning frequently, until the fish is cooked and the onions are tender. Serve sprinkled with mint leaves and accompanied by lime wedges and a salad of your choice.

mediterranean-style
plaice turbans

serves 4

each serving is:

Free on Original

Free on Extra Easy

freezer friendly

ready in 50 minutes

12 spring onions, trimmed and finely chopped

4 garlic cloves, peeled and crushed

2 red peppers, deseeded and finely diced

2 x 400g can chopped tomatoes

4 tbsp balsamic vinegar

4 tbsp sweetener

4 tsp dried herbs de Provence

salt and freshly ground black pepper

8 skinless plaice fillets

low calorie cooking spray

fresh basil leaves, to garnish

It may have an unusual name, but this is a light and attractive-looking dish that combines fillets of fresh plaice with a rich, slightly spicy tomato sauce. It's well worth the time it takes to make.

Preheat the oven to 190°C/Gas 5. Place the spring onions in a non-stick frying pan with the garlic, peppers, tomatoes, balsamic vinegar, sweetener and dried herbs. Bring to the boil and cook over a medium heat for 12-15 minutes, stirring often, until the mixture has reduced and thickened. Season.

Place the fish fillets on a clean work surface and cut each one in half, lengthways. Carefully spread half the tomato mixture along the surface of the fish. Roll up from the tail end to form a turban and secure with a cocktail stick. Repeat with the remaining fillets.

Spray a shallow ovenproof dish with low calorie cooking spray and place the rolled turbans of fish in a single layer to fit snugly. Cover lightly with foil and bake in the oven for 10-12 minutes or until the fish is cooked through.

To serve, carefully remove the fish from the ovenproof dish and place onto four plates. Remove the cocktail sticks and spoon over the remaining tomato sauce.

Garnish with the basil and serve with vegetables of your choice.

cod cakes with tartare sauce

serves 4

each serving is:

Free on Original

Free on Extra Easy

freezer friendly

ready in 50 minutes
plus chilling time

These are very special fishcakes – made with cod fillet and tiger prawns and flavoured with a subtle mix of herbs and spices. Using celeriac instead of potato keeps them Free on Original days and adds a lovely depth of flavour.

300g celeriac, peeled and cut into small pieces

2 garlic cloves, peeled

4 spring onions, trimmed and thinly sliced

a dash of Tabasco sauce

a small bunch of fresh dill

2 tsp finely grated lemon zest

250g skinless cod fillets, roughly chopped

100g raw tiger prawns, peeled

1 small egg, beaten

salt and freshly ground black pepper

low calorie cooking spray

for the tartare sauce

4 small red shallots, peeled and very finely diced

2 tbsp capers, rinsed and drained

4 tbsp chopped gherkins

1 plum tomato, deseeded and roughly chopped

200g fat free natural yogurt

Boil the celeriac in lightly salted water for 8-10 minutes until tender. Drain thoroughly and place in a food processor. Add the garlic, spring onions, Tabasco, dill, lemon zest, cod, prawns and the beaten egg. Season and process until fairly smooth.

Transfer to a bowl, cover and chill for 3-4 hours, or overnight if time permits, for the mixture to firm up and to allow the flavours to develop.

Preheat the oven to 200°C/Gas 6. Line a large baking sheet with non-stick baking parchment. Divide the fish mixture into eight portions and shape each into a ball. Flatten to form cakes and place on the baking sheet. Spray with low calorie cooking spray and bake in the oven for 15-20 minutes or until cooked through.

While the cod cakes are cooking make the sauce by combining all the ingredients in a bowl, season well and chill until ready to serve. Serve the cod cakes warm with the tartare sauce. Delicious served with a crisp salad.

luxury fish pie

serves 4

each serving is:

Free on Original

Free on Extra Easy

freezer friendly

ready in 1½ hours

for the topping

400g carrots, peeled
and roughly chopped

300g swede, peeled
and roughly chopped

1 large egg, beaten

4 tbsp fat free natural yogurt

salt and freshly ground
black pepper

for the pie

300g fat free natural yogurt

150g quark

4 tbsp chopped fresh dill

2 tbsp chopped
fresh flat-leaf parsley

200g skinless cod fillets,
cooked and cut into large
bite-sized pieces

200g skinless smoked
haddock fillets, cooked
and flaked

3 hard boiled eggs,
peeled and quartered

200g cooked
and peeled prawns

juice of ½ lemon

Ultimate comfort food, this fish pie has a carrot and swede mash topping making it Free on an Original day. It's also really easy as there's no separate sauce to make.

Start by making the topping. Put the carrots and swede in a large pan of lightly salted boiling water and cook for 25-30 minutes, until tender. Drain, return to the pan and mash. Allow to cool. Stir in the beaten egg and yogurt, season and set aside.

Preheat the oven to 200°C/Gas 6.

Place the yogurt, quark, dill and parsley in a saucepan and warm gently. Add the cod and haddock and cook for 5 minutes.

Place the quark and fish mixture in a large mixing bowl with the hard boiled eggs, prawns and lemon juice, season and mix well. Transfer this mixture to a deep, ovenproof dish. Spoon the topping over the surface, then ruffle with a fork. Place in the oven and bake for 20-25 minutes until the topping is lightly browned.

This pie is delicious served with asparagus and broccoli.

You can change the fish to suit your taste — salmon is particularly tasty.

mexican-style
prawn and pepper stir-fry

Cayenne pepper and lime add a hot, fresh flavour to this dish of prawns with sweet, tender peppers and tomatoes.

serves 4
each serving is:
Free on Original
Free on Extra Easy

ready in 40 minutes

Spray a large non-stick wok or frying pan with low calorie cooking spray and place over a medium heat. Add the garlic and spring onions, stir and cook for 2-3 minutes.

Stir in the ground cumin, cayenne, mixed peppers, tomatoes, red wine vinegar, stock and sweetener. Bring to the boil, reduce the heat and cook for 12-15 minutes, stirring occasionally.

Add the prawns to the tomato mixture. Cook over a high heat for 4-5 minutes or until the prawns turn pink and are just cooked through. Remove from the heat, squeeze over the lime wedges, season and serve.

low calorie cooking spray

3 garlic cloves, peeled and thinly sliced

8 spring onions, trimmed and thinly sliced

2 tsp ground cumin

1 tsp cayenne pepper

3 mixed peppers (orange, red and yellow) deseeded and thinly sliced

400g can chopped tomatoes

1 tbsp red wine vinegar

150ml chicken stock

2 tbsp sweetener

700g raw tiger prawns, peeled

1 lime, cut into wedges

salt and freshly ground black pepper

For an extra 'veg hit' stir in a small pack of baby leaf spinach at the end of cooking until just wilted.

seafood
stew

The fennel and spices make this a wonderfully fragrant, sophisticated dish: imagine yourself on a sunny terrace in the south of France!

serves 4

each serving is:

Free on Original

Free on Extra Easy

freezer friendly

ready in 65 minutes

1 red pepper, deseeded and roughly chopped

1 leek, trimmed and thickly sliced

1 fennel bulb, trimmed and roughly chopped

2 garlic cloves, peeled and thinly sliced

2 x 400g cans chopped tomatoes

2 tbsp sweetener

a few drops of Tabasco sauce

600ml chicken stock

1 tsp crushed fennel seeds

1 tsp dried mixed herbs

a pinch of saffron threads

1kg cooked mixed luxury seafood of your choice (eg prawns, squid, mussels)

salt and freshly ground black pepper

chopped fresh flat-leaf parsley, to garnish

Place the pepper, leek and fennel in a large non-stick saucepan. Add the garlic together with the tomatoes, sweetener, Tabasco, stock, fennel seeds, mixed herbs and saffron. Place over a high heat and bring to the boil. Reduce the heat, cover tightly and cook gently for 40 minutes, stirring occasionally.

Stir in the cooked seafood, season well and heat through for 3-4 minutes. Remove from the heat and serve immediately, garnished with chopped parsley.

Saffron is expensive, so as an alternative you can use 1/4 tsp turmeric.

fried citrus mackerel fillets

In this recipe, the mackerel is lightly fried and then left to cool, marinating in lemon juice, which finishes the 'cooking' – a classic way to serve this rich, tasty fish.

serves 4

each serving is:

Free on Original

Free on Extra Easy

ready in 20 minutes plus marinating

Season the mackerel fillets well. Spray a large non-stick frying pan with low calorie cooking spray and place over a high heat. Cook the fish, flesh side down, for 1 minute, then turn over and sear the other side for a minute. Transfer the fish carefully to a shallow ceramic dish to fit snugly in a single layer.

Wipe out the frying pan with kitchen paper and add the lemon juice, sweetener, shallots, carrot and red pepper. Bring to the boil, reduce the heat and simmer for 2 minutes. Pour this mixture over the fish. Allow to cool, cover tightly with cling film, and marinate in the fridge for 24 hours.

Remove the fish from the marinade and serve sprinkled with parsley. It tastes delicious served with a crisp green salad or green veg of your choice.

4 large mackerel fillets

salt and freshly ground black pepper

low calorie cooking spray

500ml lemon juice

2 tbsp sweetener

4 shallots, peeled and very thinly sliced

1 carrot, peeled and very finely diced

1 red pepper, deseeded and very finely diced

fresh flat-leaf parsley sprigs, to serve

salmon with parsley sauce

serves 4

each serving is:

Free on Original

Free on Extra Easy

freezer friendly

ready in about 30 minutes

This light, slightly sharp sauce complements the richness of the salmon perfectly.

4 large, skinless salmon fillets

for the sauce

100g fresh flat-leaf parsley, roughly chopped

200g fat free natural fromage frais

100g quark

100ml fish stock

4 tbsp capers, rinsed and chopped

salt and freshly ground black pepper

Make the sauce by placing the parsley, fromage frais, quark, stock and capers in a food processor and blending until smooth. Season well, transfer to a bowl and set aside until ready to serve.

Preheat the grill until hot. Place the salmon fillets on a grill rack in a single layer and season well. Grill for 8-10 minutes, or until the fish is cooked through.

Place each fillet on a plate and spoon over the sauce.

Delicious served with asparagus spears, green beans, carrots and lemon wedges to squeeze.

grilled trout with warm beetroot salsa

Trout is a wonderfully versatile fish. Here we've simply grilled it and served it with a warm beetroot salsa.

Preheat the grill to hot. Place the trout fillets on a grill rack in a single layer. Spray with low calorie cooking spray and season well. Place under the grill and cook for 8-10 minutes or until the fish is cooked through. Roughly flake and set aside.

Meanwhile spray a non-stick frying pan with low calorie cooking spray and place on a medium heat. Add the cumin, fennel and coriander seeds, and red chilli and stir-fry for 1-2 minutes. Add the beetroot, stir and cook for 2-3 minutes until warmed through.

Remove from the heat, stir in the spring onions and chopped herbs and season well. Divide the beetroot salsa between four plates or bowls and top with the flaked trout. Drizzle over the yogurt and serve immediately with lime wedges to squeeze over.

Salmon would also work well in this recipe.

serves 4

each serving is:

Free on Original

Free on Extra Easy

ready in 20 minutes

8 x 110g skinless trout fillets

low calorie cooking spray

salt and freshly ground black pepper

for the salsa

2 tsp cumin seeds

1 tsp fennel seeds

2 tsp crushed coriander seeds

1 red chilli, deseeded and finely chopped

2 packs cooked beetroot, chopped

6 spring onions, trimmed and finely sliced

a small handful of fresh mint, chopped

a very small handful of fresh coriander, chopped

fat free natural yogurt, to serve

lime wedges, to serve

poultry

There's nothing *poultry* about the
portion sizes in our hunger-busting
chicken, turkey and duck dishes!

char-grilled caribbean chicken

Succulent drumsticks with a crisp, Caribbean 'jerk seasoning' coating are popular in Jamaica. Here they are grilled, but you can barbecue them in summer, or bake them in the oven if you prefer. Team with fat free natural yogurt and a crisp green salad for a satisfying main course.

serves 4

each serving is:
Free on Original
Free on Extra Easy

freezer friendly
ready in 25-30 minutes
plus marinating

8 plump skinless
chicken drumsticks

for the 'jerk' marinade
3-4 allspice berries

1 tsp freshly grated nutmeg

1 tsp ground cinnamon

a pinch of ground cloves

½ small red onion,
peeled and finely grated

4-5 spring onions,
trimmed and finely sliced

1 red chilli, deseeded
and finely chopped

finely grated zest and
juice of 1 large lime

salt and freshly ground
black pepper

fat free natural yogurt,
red chilli flakes and lime
wedges, to serve

For the marinade, put the allspice berries in a small, dry, non-stick frying pan and place over a medium heat for 3-4 minutes, shaking the pan frequently, until the berries give off an aroma. Remove from the heat and place in a large mortar. Add the nutmeg, cinnamon and cloves, and grind with a pestle to a powder.

Add the red onion, spring onions, red chilli, lime zest and juice, and season to taste. Pound the mixture to a thick paste.

Cut the chicken flesh several times with a sharp knife and rub the 'jerk' marinade all over them. Place in a shallow ceramic dish, cover and marinate in the fridge for at least 1 hour or up to 24 hours.

When ready to cook, preheat the grill to high. Place the drumsticks on the grill rack and cook under the grill for 15-20 minutes, turning occasionally, until cooked through. To test whether the chicken is cooked, insert a thin metal skewer or knife tip into the thickest part and check that the juices run clear.

Serve the drumsticks hot, with fat free natural yogurt sprinkled with chilli flakes and lime wedges to squeeze over, with a salad of your choice.

These drumsticks are also delicious served cold at picnics.

thai-style
aromatic chicken stir-fry

serves 4

each serving is:

Free on Original

Free on Extra Easy

ready in 30 minutes

low calorie cooking spray

4 skinless and boneless chicken breasts, cut into thin strips

2 tbsp very finely chopped lemon grass

4cm piece root ginger, peeled and finely grated

2 garlic cloves, peeled and crushed

1 red chilli, deseeded and finely chopped

2-3 lime leaves, very finely shredded (optional)

finely grated zest and juice of 1 lime

1 red pepper, deseeded and cut into thin strips

100g mangetout, halved lengthways

1 cucumber, deseeded and cut into thin strips

1 carrot, peeled and cut into thin strips

100ml chicken stock

3 tbsp soy sauce

chopped fresh coriander leaves

This quick and flavour-packed stir-fry of tender chicken strips and vegetables is best cooked minutes before you sit down to eat.

Spray a large non-stick wok or frying pan with low calorie cooking spray and heat until hot. Add the chicken and stir-fry over a high heat for 4-5 minutes, until just cooked through. Remove with a slotted spoon and keep warm.

Re-spray the pan with low calorie cooking spray and add the lemon grass, ginger, garlic, red chilli, lime leaves, lime zest and juice, red pepper, mangetout, cucumber and carrot. Stir-fry over a high heat for 3-4 minutes and then return the chicken to the pan with the stock and soy sauce. Cook for 2-3 minutes and scatter over the coriander leaves.

This dish goes particularly well with pak choi or shredded cabbage.

Turkey would also work well in this dish and halved baby sweetcorn makes a great veg alternative.

mediterranean
chicken hot pot

serves 4

each serving is:

Free on Original

Free on Extra Easy

freezer friendly

ready in 2 hours 5 minutes

Slow cooking the chicken and vegetables in this casserole creates a deliciously fragrant, meltingly tender dish that will become an instant family favourite.

6 large skinless chicken breast fillets, cut into bite-sized pieces

400g can tomatoes

3 garlic cloves, peeled and finely chopped

6 shallots, peeled and halved

1 red pepper, deseeded and cut into bite-sized pieces

1 yellow pepper deseeded and cut into bite-sized pieces

2 courgettes, thickly sliced

200g mushrooms, thickly sliced

1 tsp dried mixed herbs

1 tbsp sweetener

700ml chicken stock

salt and freshly ground black pepper

a large handful of fresh basil leaves, to serve

Preheat the oven to 200°C/Gas 6. Place the chicken in a medium casserole dish with the canned tomatoes.

Add the garlic to the chicken mixture with the shallots, peppers, courgettes, mushrooms, dried mixed herbs, sweetener and chicken stock.

Place the casserole dish over a high heat and bring to the boil. Cover very tightly, place in the oven and cook for 1½ hours.

Remove from the oven, season well and stir in the basil leaves just before serving.

sweet and sour chicken

Enjoy the flavours of sweet and sour chicken without the sticky heaviness of a restaurant version – it's just as quick as a takeaway too.

Place the chicken in a shallow ceramic dish. Sprinkle over the spring onions and garlic, season well and pour over the light soy sauce. Toss to mix well, cover and marinate in the fridge for 30 minutes.

Spray a large non-stick frying pan with low calorie cooking spray and place over a high heat. Add the chicken mixture and cook for 5-6 minutes and then add the dark soy sauce, sweetener, vinegar, paprika, 5-spice powder and passata. Stir to mix well and bring the mixture to the boil.

Reduce the heat and cook gently for 3-4 minutes or until the chicken is cooked through. Check the seasoning before serving garnished with spring onion slivers and lime wedges to squeeze over.

This dish would also work brilliantly with pork.

serves 4

each serving is:

Free on Original

Free on Extra Easy

ready in 25 minutes plus marinating

6 skinless chicken breast fillets, very thinly sliced

6 spring onions, trimmed and finely sliced

2 garlic cloves, peeled and finely chopped

salt and freshly ground black pepper

3 tbsp light soy sauce

low calorie cooking spray

1 tbsp dark soy sauce

2 tbsp sweetener

1 tbsp balsamic vinegar

1 tsp paprika

½ tsp Chinese 5-spice powder

100ml passata

spring onion slivers and lime wedges, to garnish

chicken tikka masala

serves 4

each serving is:

Free on Original

Free on Extra Easy

freezer friendly

ready in 45 minutes

6 skinless chicken breast fillets

low calorie cooking spray

salt and freshly ground black pepper

2 large shallots, peeled and finely grated

3 garlic cloves, peeled and finely grated

½ tsp crushed cardamom seeds

½ tsp turmeric

1 tbsp tikka masala powder or tandoori spice blend powder

4 tbsp passata

150ml chicken stock

100g fat free natural fromage frais

tomato and red onion slices, to garnish

Your local Indian restaurant will wonder what's happened to you once you've discovered this fantastic home-made version of a classic Indian dish that's completely Free on an Original day.

Spray the chicken with low calorie cooking spray and season well. Place under a preheated hot grill and cook for 15-20 minutes, turning once until cooked through. Remove and, when cool, cut into bite-sized pieces. Set aside.

Spray a large non-stick frying pan with low calorie cooking spray and place over a medium heat. Add the shallots and garlic along with the crushed cardamom seeds, turmeric and tikka masala powder. Stir-fry for 1 minute before adding the passata.

Add the chicken and stock and cook for 4-5 minutes, stirring often. Remove from the heat, stir in the fromage frais and season to taste. Garnish with the tomato and red onion slices.

Great served with cabbage sprinkled with black onion seeds.

creamy chicken korma

This favourite dish is a takeaway classic, loved for its mild, yet fragrant flavour. Traditionally you'd use cream in a korma – here we use fromage frais to give the creamy taste without the Syns.

serves 4

each serving is:

Free on Original

Free on Extra Easy

freezer friendly

ready in 45 minutes

Spray a large frying pan with low calorie cooking spray and place over a high heat. Add the bay leaves, cinnamon stick, cardamom pods, cloves, cumin seeds and onion and stir-fry for 5-6 minutes.

Add the ground coriander and cumin, ginger, garlic, tomatoes and korma curry powder and stir-fry for another 3-4 minutes.

Add the chicken to the pan and pour over the stock. Bring to the boil and season well. Cover tightly, reduce the heat to low and allow to simmer gently for 20-25 minutes, stirring occasionally.

Remove the pan from the heat, stir in the fromage frais and garnish with mint.

This is delicious served with a salad of chopped red onion and tomato, and drizzled with fat free fromage frais.

low calorie cooking spray

3 bay leaves

1 cinnamon stick

2 tsp cardamom pods, lightly crushed

¼ tsp crushed cloves

2 tsp cumin seeds

1 onion, peeled and finely grated

1 tbsp ground coriander

1 tbsp ground cumin

6cm piece root ginger, peeled and finely grated

3 garlic cloves, peeled and finely crushed

200g can chopped tomatoes

2 tsp korma curry powder

6 skinless and boneless chicken breasts, cut into bite-sized pieces

200ml chicken stock

salt and freshly ground black pepper

5 tbsp fat free natural fromage frais

fresh mint leaves, to garnish

garlicky
chicken casserole

serves 4

each serving is:

Free on Original

Free on Extra Easy

freezer friendly

ready in 45 minutes

low calorie cooking spray

800g skinless chicken breast fillets, cut into bite-sized pieces

2 onions, peeled and roughly chopped

2 large carrots, peeled and cut into thick batons

1 bulb of garlic, separated but not peeled

400ml chicken stock

4-5 fresh tarragon sprigs

salt and freshly ground black pepper

200g green beans, trimmed and halved

fresh tarragon, to garnish

This classic dish is perfect for relaxed entertaining as it can be made ahead of time and simply reheated before serving.

Spray a large non-stick casserole dish with low calorie cooking spray and place over a high heat. Add the chicken pieces and cook until lightly browned on all sides.

Add the onions, carrots, garlic, stock and tarragon, season well and bring to the boil. Reduce the heat, cover with a lid and cook gently for 20 minutes.

Five minutes before the end of the cooking time add the green beans.

Check the seasoning and remove any rogue garlic skins before serving sprinkled with tarragon sprigs.

You can leave the cloves of garlic whole, or once cooked, use a fork to mash them into the casserole sauce.

creamy chicken, apple and celery salad

This refreshing salad of chicken, apple and celery can be used in lunchboxes or as part of a picnic.

serves 4
each serving is:
Free on Original
Free on Extra Easy

ready in 10 minutes

Place the chicken in a large salad bowl with the apples, celery, spinach, spring onions and chives.

To make the dressing, mix all the ingredients together in a bowl. Pour over the salad ingredients and toss to mix well.

Scatter over the chopped egg and chives before serving.

6 cooked, skinless chicken breasts, cut into bite-sized chunks

4 red apples, cored and cut into bite-sized chunks

4 celery sticks, trimmed and thinly sliced

25g baby leaf spinach

6 spring onions, trimmed and thinly sliced

a bunch of fresh chives, chopped

2 hard boiled eggs, peeled and finely chopped, to garnish

chopped fresh chives, to garnish

for the dressing
200g fat free natural fromage frais

3 tbsp fat free salad dressing

2 tbsp chopped gherkins

salt and freshly ground black pepper

turkey roll
with spinach and peppers

serves 4-6

each serving is:

Free on Original

Free on Extra Easy

freezer friendly

ready in about
1 hour 25 minutes

This easy, make-ahead Italian-style boneless turkey joint will have your family or guests saying 'grazie'.

500g turkey breast joint

salt and freshly ground black pepper

4 slices lean Wiltshire ham

450g jar roasted red peppers in brine, drained

low calorie cooking spray

1 onion, peeled and finely chopped

2 tbsp chopped fresh thyme leaves, plus extra for garnish

2 x 250g bags baby leaf spinach

1 large leek, trimmed and thinly sliced

300ml hot chicken stock

2 fat cloves garlic, unpeeled

2-3 tbsp fat free natural fromage frais

a small handful of fresh flat-leaf parsley, chopped

Preheat the oven to 200°C/Gas 6. Discard the skin from the turkey breast. Place the breast on a chopping board lined with cling film. Cover the meat with a piece of cling film and bash with a rolling pin or meat mallet to flatten slightly. If necessary cut a thin slice off the thickest part of the turkey breast and add to the thinnest part to even out the flattened meat – it should be about 23cm square. Season well with salt and pepper and cover with the sliced ham.

Open out the peppers and discard any seeds and arrange over the ham in a single layer.

Spray a saucepan with low calorie cooking spray and place the onion, half of the thyme and 100ml of water in the pan. Bring to the boil and simmer for 5 minutes until the water has evaporated. Stir in the spinach and cook gently until wilted.

Spread the spinach mixture thinly over the red peppers. Roll up tightly like a Swiss roll cake and tie at intervals with string.

Place in a roasting tin, spray with low calorie cooking spray and scatter with the remaining thyme. Pour half of the stock into the roasting tin and scatter over the garlic cloves. Roast for 1 hour.

Meanwhile place the remaining stock into a small saucepan with the leek and simmer gently for 10 minutes.

Remove the meat from the roasting tin and pop the garlic cloves from their papery skins. Add the garlic to the leek mixture along with the pan juices and purée with a stick blender. Stir in the fromage frais and chopped parsley and serve spooned over the sliced meat. Garnish with the remaining thyme leaves and serve with green veg of your choice.

turkey with pesto and roasted veg

Pesto sauce can be very high in Syns but our version is completely Free and has just as much flavour. It's the perfect partner for meaty turkey steaks.

First make the pesto. Place the garlic in a food processor with the basil and parsley. Add the balsamic vinegar, Worcestershire sauce and stock and blitz until fairly smooth. Add a little more stock if the mixture is too thick to process smoothly (it's best to use a small food processor). Season and transfer to a bowl and set aside until needed.

Preheat the oven to 200°C/Gas 6 and line a large baking sheet with non-stick baking parchment.

Place the vegetables on the baking sheet, spray with low calorie cooking spray and roast in the oven for 30-35 minutes.

Meanwhile preheat a ridged griddle until just smoking. Spray each turkey breast on both sides with low calorie cooking spray and season well. Char-grill the steaks for 2-3 minutes on one side, then turn over and char-grill for a further 2 minutes.

Serve the turkey with the roasted vegetables, pour over the pesto sauce and sprinkle with basil leaves.

If you haven't got a griddle, the turkey will be just as delicious grilled.

serves 4

each serving is:

Free on Original

Free on Extra Easy

freezer friendly (not the pesto)
ready in 45 minutes

4 skinless turkey breast steaks

fresh basil leaves, to garnish

for the pesto

3 garlic cloves, peeled and finely grated

8 tbsp very finely chopped fresh basil

4 tbsp very finely chopped fresh flat-leaf parsley

2 tbsp balsamic vinegar

1 tbsp Worcestershire sauce

125ml chicken stock

salt and freshly ground black pepper

for the vegetables

2 large courgettes, trimmed and cut into chunks

3 mixed peppers (green, red and yellow), deseeded and cut into chunks

1 large onion, peeled and cut into wedges

low calorie cooking spray

duck, mango
and watercress salad

serves 4

each serving is:

Free on Original

Free on Extra Easy

ready in 30-35 minutes

4 skinless duck breasts,
all visible fat removed

salt and freshly ground
black pepper

low calorie cooking spray

2 ripe sweet mangoes

4 spring onions, trimmed
and shredded

1 red pepper, deseeded
and very thinly sliced

a large bunch of watercress

for the dressing

4 tbsp light soy sauce

1 tsp Chinese 5-spice powder

1 tbsp Worcestershire sauce

1 tsp Tabasco sauce

60ml chicken stock

Peppery watercress, sweet mango, rich duck breast and crunchy red pepper combine in a luxury salad with a tropical tang.

Season the duck breasts well and spray with low calorie cooking spray. Place on a grill rack under a preheated medium-hot grill for 6-8 minutes on each side or until cooked to your liking. Remove from the grill, cover with foil and allow to rest for 10 minutes.

Meanwhile, peel, stone and cut the mangoes into thin slices and place in a large bowl with the spring onions, red pepper and watercress. Toss to mix well.

To serve, divide the salad mixture between four serving plates. Thinly slice the duck and place on top of the salad. Mix together all the dressing ingredients and serve the salad with the dressing spooned over.

lamb

Spoil yourself with this
luscious selection of tender
lamb dishes.

lamb kebabs
with aubergine purée

In the summer, try cooking these delicious kebabs on the barbecue for an extra special flavour. If you like a citrus kick try adding lemon wedges to the skewers before cooking.

serves 4

each serving is:

Free on Original

Free on Extra Easy

freezer friendly

ready in 45 minutes plus marinating

350g lean lamb fillets, all visible fat removed, cut into bite-sized pieces

2 red peppers, deseeded and cut into bite-sized pieces

for the marinade

3 garlic cloves, peeled and crushed

2 tbsp chopped fresh rosemary leaves

juice of 1 lemon

100g fat free natural yogurt

2 tsp finely grated lemon zest

salt and freshly ground black pepper

for the purée

2 large aubergines

1 garlic clove, peeled and crushed

6 spring onions, finely chopped

juice of 1 lemon

8-9 tbsp finely chopped fresh mint

6 plum tomatoes, deseeded and finely chopped

Put the lamb in a mixing bowl. Mix together the marinade ingredients, add to the lamb, season and toss. Cover and leave to marinate for a few hours in the fridge.

Preheat the oven to 220°C/Gas 7. Prick the aubergine skins all over with a fork, place on a non-stick baking sheet and bake for 25-30 minutes or until the aubergines are soft. Remove and cover with foil until cool enough to handle.

To make the purée, halve the aubergines and scoop the flesh into a food processor. Add the garlic, spring onions, lemon juice and chopped mint. Season and blend until fairly smooth. Transfer to a bowl and stir in the tomatoes. Set aside.

Preheat the grill to hot. Thread the lamb and red pepper pieces onto eight skewers and grill for 7-8 minutes, turning once, until browned. To serve, place two kebabs on each plate with a portion of the purée and accompany with salad of your choice.

Sliced courgettes would also work well on the skewers.

mustard and garlic-roasted leg of lamb

serves 4-6

each serving is:

Free on Original

Free on Extra Easy

freezer friendly

ready in 1¾ hours
plus resting

1 small leg of lamb,
weighing about 3kg,
all visible fat removed

3 tbsp mustard powder

10 garlic cloves, peeled

a small bunch
rosemary sprigs

sea salt and freshly
ground black pepper

2 courgettes, sliced

1 red pepper, deseeded
and cut into chunks

1 yellow pepper, deseeded
and cut into chunks

1 bulb of garlic,
sliced horizontally

Rosemary is a classic flavour to accompany lamb, and here it's given an extra boost with mustard and garlic. Perfect for a special Sunday lunch.

Preheat the oven to 230°C/Gas 8.

Rub the leg of lamb all over with the mustard powder. Cut each garlic clove into 3-4 long slivers and, using a short sharp knife, make small cuts in the flesh of the lamb and stud with the garlic and small sprigs of rosemary, saving some to sprinkle over the veg. Season liberally with salt and freshly ground black pepper.

Place in a roasting tin with the vegetables and remaining rosemary. Put in the oven for 10-12 minutes per 500g for rare lamb or 15 minutes per 500g for medium. After the first 15 minutes reduce the heat to 180°C/Gas 4. Baste the meat from time to time with the pan juices.

When ready, remove from the oven and allow the lamb to rest, covered in foil, in a warm place for 15-20 minutes before carving and serving with the roasted veg.

luxury
shepherd's pie

Our version of this traditional dish is completely Free on an Original day. Comfort food doesn't get any better than this!

Cook the swede in a saucepan of boiling water until tender, about 8-10 minutes. Drain, return to the pan and mash until smooth. Stir in the yogurt and parsley, season well and set aside until needed.

Meanwhile spray a large frying pan with low calorie cooking spray and place over a high heat. Add the onion, garlic, celery and carrots and stir-fry for 4-5 minutes.

Add the lamb and stir-fry for 4-5 minutes. Stir in the tomatoes, sweetener and oregano and crumble the stock cube over, bring to the boil and remove from the heat.

Preheat the oven to 200°C/Gas 6. Transfer the lamb mixture to a large dish (or four individual ones) and top with the swede, swirling with a fork to ruffle up the surface. Brush the top with the beaten egg and bake for 25-30 minutes, until lightly golden and bubbling. Serve with veg of your choice.

You can also use butternut squash or a mixture of carrot and swede for the topping.

serves 4
each serving is:
Free on Original
Free on Extra Easy

freezer friendly
ready in 1 hour 10 minutes

900g swede,
peeled and chopped

6 tbsp fat free natural yogurt

4 tbsp chopped
fresh flat-leaf parsley

salt and freshly ground
black pepper

low calorie cooking spray

1 red onion, peeled
and finely chopped

2 garlic cloves, peeled
and finely chopped

2 celery sticks,
finely chopped

2 carrots, peeled
and finely chopped

500g extra lean lamb,
minced

400g can chopped tomatoes

1 tsp sweetener

2 tsp dried oregano

1 beef stock cube

1 egg, beaten

aromatic
lamb tagine

serves 4

each serving is:

Free on Original

Free on Extra Easy

freezer friendly

ready in 1 hour 20 minutes

low calorie cooking spray

1 onion, peeled
and finely chopped

2 tsp ground cumin

2 tsp ground cinnamon

350g lean lamb steaks,
all visible fat removed,
cut into bite-sized pieces

400g can chopped tomatoes

2 tsp sweetener

300g swede, peeled and
cut into 1.5cm pieces

400g carrots, peeled and
cut into 1.5cm pieces

salt and freshly ground
black pepper

chopped fresh coriander,
to garnish

You can put almost anything into a tagine! Here we've used lean lamb and chunks of carrot and swede to produce a warming, comforting dish.

Spray a large frying pan with low calorie cooking spray and place over a high heat. Add the onion, cumin, cinnamon and lamb and stir-fry for 5-6 minutes.

Add the tomatoes and sweetener and bring to the boil. Lower the heat, then cover and simmer gently for 35-40 minutes, stirring often, or until the meat is tender.

Stir in the swede and carrots and cook for a further 15 minutes, or until the vegetables are tender. Season well and serve garnished with chopped coriander and veg of your choice.

one pot lamb shanks

This meaty cut from the lower end of the leg is full of flavour – it becomes meltingly tender and falls from the bone after long, slow cooking. This hearty and delicious dish is perfect for easy entertaining as it's cooked in one pot.

serves 4
each serving is:
Free on Original
Free on Extra Easy

freezer friendly
ready in 3 hours
plus standing

Spray a heavy, non-stick casserole dish with low calorie cooking spray and place over a high heat. Add the lamb and lightly brown on all sides. Remove the shanks with a slotted spoon and set aside.

Lower the heat to medium and add the onion, carrots, celery and garlic to the dish. Stir-fry for 10 minutes, then add the tomatoes, stock, sweetener (if using) and bay leaf. Season well.

Return the shanks to the dish, stir and cover tightly. Reduce the heat to very low and cook for 2½ hours, stirring occasionally, until the meat is meltingly tender. Discard the bay leaf and allow to stand for 10 minutes before serving sprinkled with parsley.

low calorie cooking spray

4 lamb shanks,
all visible fat removed

1 onion, peeled
and finely chopped

2 carrots, peeled
and finely chopped

2 celery sticks, trimmed
and finely chopped

4 garlic cloves, peeled
and finely chopped

400g can chopped tomatoes

200ml lamb stock

1 tsp sweetener (optional)

1 bay leaf

salt and freshly ground
black pepper

finely chopped fresh
flat-leaf parsley, to serve

lamb rogan josh

Seasoned with fragrant spices, this slow cooked curry produces lamb that's meltingly tender – a treat for all the senses.

serves 4

each serving is:

Free on Original

Free on Extra Easy

freezer friendly

ready in 2¾ hours

low calorie cooking spray

800g boneless lamb shoulder, all visible fat removed, cut into large bite-sized pieces

2 onions, peeled, halved and thickly sliced

4 garlic cloves, peeled and crushed

2cm piece root ginger, peeled and finely grated

2 cinnamon sticks

4 tsp paprika

2 tsp crushed cardamom seeds

4 tbsp medium curry powder

400g can chopped tomatoes

1 tsp sweetener

600ml lamb stock

600g swede, peeled and cut into large pieces

salt and freshly ground black pepper

chopped fresh coriander and fat free natural yogurt, to serve

Spray a large, heavy-based casserole or saucepan with low calorie cooking spray and cook the lamb in batches for 3-4 minutes, until browned. Remove with a slotted spoon and set aside.

Spray the casserole again and add the onions. Cook over a medium heat for 10-12 minutes, stirring often, until soft and lightly browned.

Add the garlic, ginger, cinnamon, paprika and cardamom seeds and stir-fry for 1-2 minutes. Mix in the curry powder. Return the lamb to the casserole and stir-fry for a further 2-3 minutes. Stir in the tomatoes, sweetener, stock and swede. Season well and bring to the boil.

Reduce the heat to very low and cover tightly. Simmer gently for 2 hours, or until the lamb is meltingly tender. Serve garnished with chopped coriander and drizzled with yogurt.

liver
and bacon with onions

The wonderful fragrance of fresh sage transforms this traditional dish of liver and bacon into something special.

serves 4

each serving is:

Free on Original

Free on Extra Easy

freezer friendly

ready in 20-25 minutes

Rinse the liver, drain and pat dry with kitchen paper. Season well with salt and pepper and set aside.

Place a large, non-stick frying pan over a medium heat and spray with low calorie cooking spray. Add the onion and sage and stir-fry for 4-5 minutes or until soft and lightly browned. Add the stock and bring to the boil, then lower the heat and leave to simmer gently.

Place another large, non-stick frying pan on a moderate heat and spray with low calorie cooking spray. Add the bacon and stir-fry for 1-2 minutes, then remove with a slotted spoon and reserve. Add the liver to the pan and fry over a moderate heat for 2 minutes on each side or until lightly browned.

Add the bacon and liver to the stock mixture and simmer gently for 3-4 minutes or until the liver is cooked but still slightly pink in the centre. Serve with veg of your choice.

350g lamb's liver slices

salt and freshly ground black pepper

low calorie cooking spray

1 large onion, peeled and thinly sliced

6-8 fresh sage leaves, finely shredded

300ml lamb stock

4 lean, rindless bacon rashers, all visible fat removed, roughly chopped

beef

Packed with filling power,
you'll love these hearty,
healthy beef recipes.

serves 4

each serving is:

Free on Original

Free on Extra Easy

freezer friendly

ready in 25 minutes
plus marinating

450g thick beef fillet steaks,
all visible fat removed

for the marinade

4 tbsp light soy sauce

2 garlic cloves,
peeled and crushed

4 tbsp finely chopped
lemon grass

1 tbsp sweetener

1-2 chillies, deseeded
and finely chopped

2cm piece root ginger,
peeled and finely grated

1 tsp finely grated lime zest

juice of 3 limes

for the salad

1 large carrot,
peeled and grated

4 little gem lettuces,
trimmed and washed

1 small cucumber,
deseeded and thinly sliced

60g bean sprouts

4 spring onions, trimmed
and finely shredded

4 tbsp roughly chopped
fresh coriander

2 tbsp chopped fresh mint

for the dressing

3 tbsp soy sauce

½ finely chopped red chilli

juice of 2 limes

1 tbsp sweetener

salt and freshly ground
black pepper

spicy
thai-style beef salad

Fragrant with Far Eastern herbs, this is a substantial
salad of beef with crisp and crunchy vegetables.

Place the steaks in a shallow mixing bowl. Mix together the marinade
ingredients and pour over the steaks. Cover and leave to marinate in the
fridge for a few hours, or overnight if time permits.

Place all the salad ingredients in a large bowl. In a separate smaller bowl,
mix all the dressing ingredients together and season to taste. Pour over the
salad and toss to mix.

Preheat the grill to hot and then remove the steaks from the marinade. Place
on a grill rack and cook for 4-5 minutes on each side, or until cooked to your
liking. Remove, cover and leave to rest for 5 minutes before cutting into very
thin slices. Divide the salad mixture between four plates, top with the beef
steaks and serve immediately.

creamy beef goulash

serves 4-6

each serving is:

Free on Original

Free on Extra Easy

freezer friendly

ready in 2 hours 10 minutes

400g can chopped tomatoes

1 large onion, peeled and finely chopped

300g chestnut mushrooms, sliced

2 red peppers, deseeded and diced

1kg lean braising steak, all visible fat removed, cut into thin strips

2 tbsp smoked paprika

½ tsp caraway seeds

1 bay leaf

a pinch of marjoram

1 tsp dried mixed herbs

salt and freshly ground black pepper

250g fat fee natural fromage frais

Smoked paprika gives an extra depth to the spicy flavour of this winter warmer, but standard paprika works well too.

Preheat the oven to 150°C/Gas 2. Put the tomatoes and onion in a saucepan and place over a medium heat. Bring to the boil, reduce the heat and cook gently for 10-12 minutes, until the onions have softened.

Stir in the mushrooms and peppers and cook for a further 6-8 minutes.

Place the steak in an ovenproof dish. Sprinkle over the paprika, caraway seeds, bay leaf, marjoram and dried herbs. Season well and pour over the tomato mixture. Cover tightly and cook in the oven for 1½ hours or until the meat is tender.

Beat the fromage frais until smooth and pour over the casserole before serving. Cabbage and carrots would make a perfect accompaniment.

This recipe would also work well with pork or lamb.

daube
of beef

serves 4

each serving is:

Free on Original

Free on Extra Easy

freezer friendly

ready in 2½ hours

A daube is a classic French stew using beef. This version is really hearty with chunky vegetables, just perfect for supper on a cold winter night.

low calorie cooking spray

700g lean stewing beef, all visible fat removed, cut into bite-sized pieces

2 garlic cloves, peeled and crushed

2 onions, peeled and roughly chopped

3 carrots, peeled and roughly chopped

1 medium turnip OR swede, peeled and cut into cubes

600ml beef stock

salt and freshly ground black pepper

2 tsp dried mixed herbs

chopped fresh flat-leaf parsley, to garnish

Preheat the oven to 170°C/Gas 3. Spray a large non-stick frying pan with low calorie cooking spray and place over a medium heat. Add the meat and stir-fry until brown on all sides.

Transfer the meat to a medium casserole dish with the garlic, onions, carrots, turnip or swede and stock. Season well and add the dried mixed herbs. Cover tightly and cook in the oven for 2 hours.

Serve piping hot, sprinkled with the chopped parsley.

This dish would cook beautifully in a slow cooker for around 8 hours — the meat just melts in your mouth!

beef madras

Madras curries originate from the east coast of southern India and are usually very spicy and robust in flavour – not for the faint-hearted! This recipe uses lean beef, but you can use lamb if you prefer.

Spray a saucepan liberally with low calorie cooking spray and place over a medium heat. Add the onion, cloves and cardamom pods and stir-fry for 3-4 minutes.

Add the fresh chilli, ginger, garlic and dried chilli and stir-fry for a further 2 minutes.

Add the curry powder and beef chunks to the saucepan and stir-fry for 6-8 minutes until the meat is sealed.

Add the ground coriander, cumin and stock and bring to the boil. Season with salt, cover tightly and reduce the heat to low. Cook gently for 1½ hours, stirring occasionally, until the meat is tender.

Remove the pan from the heat and scatter over some chopped coriander before serving.

This is delicious served with a cucumber, carrot and black onion seed salad.

serves 4

each serving is:

Free on Original

Free on Extra Easy

freezer friendly

ready in 2 hours

low calorie cooking spray

1 onion, peeled and finely chopped

4 cloves

6 green cardamom pods

2 fresh red chillies, finely chopped

2cm piece root ginger, peeled and finely grated

2 garlic cloves, peeled and crushed

2 dried red chillies

1 tbsp madras curry powder

900g lean beef, all visible fat removed, cut into bite-sized chunks

2 tsp ground coriander

1 tsp ground cumin

250ml beef stock

salt

chopped fresh coriander, to serve

beefed-up burgers

serves 4

each serving is:

Free on Original

Free on Extra Easy

freezer friendly

ready in 25 minutes

2 large onions, peeled and finely chopped

4 garlic cloves, peeled and finely chopped

a handful of fresh flat-leaf parsley, finely chopped

700g extra lean minced beef

8 tsp Worcestershire sauce

salt and freshly ground black pepper

This recipe turns a barbecue favourite into a super-healthy treat without compromising on taste. Fun to make, they're perfect for getting the whole family involved and they freeze brilliantly too!

Place the onions, garlic, parsley, minced beef and Worcestershire sauce in a bowl and use your hands to combine thoroughly. Season and shape into burgers.

Place each burger on a preheated barbecue and cook for 5-6 minutes on each side or until done to your liking.

Serve with a salad of your choice.

For a spicy hit add a finely diced, deseeded red chilli to the mixture.

meatloaf with spinach and pepper stuffing

Meatloaf is a classic family favourite. This particular version has a middle layer of spinach and red pepper and is served with a tasty tomato sauce. It tastes great hot or cold and makes great picnic food.

serves 4

each serving is:

Free on Original

Free on Extra Easy

freezer friendly
(only if spinach fresh)

ready in 1 hours 20 minutes
plus standing

Preheat the oven to 190°C/Gas 5. Line a large 900g loaf tin with baking parchment.

Place the onion and minced beef in a mixing bowl with the parsley, seasoning and the egg yolk. Mix well until combined.

Divide the beef mixture in half and press half into the bottom of the tin. Make an indentation down the centre of the beef and lay the spinach and peppers down its length. Top with the remaining beef, packing it down really firmly.

Cover the top of the tin with a layer of baking parchment and then foil. Bake for 1 hour or until tender and cooked through, and the juices run clear when a skewer is inserted into the middle. Stand for 10 minutes and then drain away any juices.

While the meatloaf is standing, pour the passata into a small saucepan with the garlic, stock and basil. Season and bring to the boil. Cook for 6-8 minutes or until slightly reduced and thickened.

Carefully remove the loaf from the tin and garnish with the tomatoes and basil leaves. Serve in slices with the tomato sauce to accompany.

1 small onion, peeled
and finely chopped

700g extra lean minced beef

4 tbsp chopped
fresh flat-leaf parsley

salt and freshly ground
black pepper

1 medium egg yolk

110g frozen chopped
spinach, thawed and drained
of all excess water OR 100g
baby leaf spinach, wilted

1 small red pepper,
halved, deseeded and
cut into thin strips

quartered cherry tomatoes
and fresh basil leaves,
to garnish

for the sauce

300ml passata

2 garlic cloves,
peeled and crushed

100ml vegetable stock

4 tbsp finely chopped
fresh basil

roast rib of beef
with roasted roots

Here we have the ultimate Sunday lunch in one pan, and roasting the vegetables with the meat means it's easy to have everything ready at the same time.

serves 4

each serving is:

Free on Original

Free on Extra Easy

freezer friendly

ready in 1½-2 hours
plus resting

1.2kg rib of beef joint,
all visible fat removed

1 tbsp mustard powder

2 tbsp passata

3 tbsp mixed peppercorns,
crushed

400g swede, peeled
and cut into thick pieces

500g celeriac, peeled
and cut into thick pieces

3 large carrots, peeled
and cut into thick batons

Preheat the oven to 220°C/Gas 7. Place the beef in a large, non-stick roasting tin. Mix the mustard powder with the passata until smooth and spread over the beef. Press the crushed peppercorns over this, coating evenly. Place the beef in the oven and roast for 20 minutes, then reduce the heat to 190°C/Gas 5 and roast for a further 30 minutes for rare, 45 minutes for medium rare or 1 hour for well done.

Meanwhile put the vegetables in a large saucepan of lightly salted boiling water and cook for 10 minutes. Drain and add to the roasting tin about 20 minutes before the end of the beef's cooking time.

When the beef is cooked to your liking, remove from the oven, cover and allow to rest for 10-15 minutes before carving. Serve with the roasted vegetables.

pork

You'll be spoiled for choice with
these versatile, flavourful,
Free Food-packed meals…

grilled gammon steaks
with tomatoes and herb mash

serves 4

each serving is:

Free on Original

Free on Extra Easy

freezer friendly

ready in 25 minutes

Juicy gammon steaks are grilled with flavourful vine tomatoes and served with a deliciously creamy swede mash for an excellent casual supper.

for the mash

500g swede, peeled and roughly cut into small chunks

6 spring onions, trimmed and finely chopped

3 level tbsp chopped fresh flat-leaf parsley

2 level tbsp chopped fresh basil

100g fat free natural fromage frais

fresh basil leaves, to garnish

for the gammon

4 lean smoked gammon steaks, all visible fat removed

8-12 plum tomatoes on the vine, halved

salt and freshly ground black pepper

First prepare the mash. Cook the swede in a saucepan of boiling water for 12-15 minutes until tender.

Meanwhile mix the spring onions, chopped herbs and fromage frais together in a bowl.

Preheat the grill. Lay the gammon steaks on a foil-lined large grill pan and place the tomatoes around them. Season and grill for 6-8 minutes, turning the steaks halfway through grilling.

When the swede is cooked, drain it thoroughly, then mash. Add the fromage frais mixture and combine well. Season and keep warm.

To serve, place the gammon steaks on four plates with the grilled tomatoes. Spoon the herb mash alongside and serve garnished with basil leaves.

To vary the flavour of the mash, try using butternut squash or carrot in place of the swede.

all-day
breakfast salad

This clever recipe combines the key ingredients of a cooked breakfast with salad, making a surprisingly substantial meal for any time of the day!

serves 4

each serving is:

Free on Original

Free on Extra Easy

ready in 30 minutes

for the salad

low calorie cooking spray

250g baby button mushrooms, halved

12 lean bacon rashers, all visible fat removed

4 plum tomatoes, cut into wedges

2 little gem lettuces, leaves roughly torn

4 hard boiled eggs, peeled and roughly chopped

3 tbsp chopped fresh chives

for the dressing

100g fat free natural fromage frais

100ml passata

1 tsp mustard powder mixed with 2 tsp water

salt and freshly ground black pepper

Spray a large non-stick frying pan with low calorie cooking spray and add the mushrooms. Cook over a high heat for 3-4 minutes or until the mushrooms are tender and lightly browned. Transfer to a salad bowl.

Add the bacon to the frying pan and cook for 3-4 minutes on each side or until crisp and lightly browned. Drain on kitchen paper, then cut into bite-sized pieces and add to the mushrooms.

Add the tomatoes and lettuce leaves to the salad ingredients. Sprinkle the chopped eggs on top of the salad and add the chives.

Make the dressing by mixing all the ingredients together in a bowl.

To serve, divide the salad mixture between four plates and drizzle over the dressing.

pork and herb meatballs
with ratatouille sauce

These herby lean pork meatballs are grilled and served on a bed of rich and colourful Mediterranean veg. Use beef as an alternative if you prefer.

Place the spring onions in a mixing bowl and add the pork, dried herbs and plenty of seasoning. Mix well to combine and then divide into 20 portions. Form into small balls and place on a plate lined with baking parchment. Cover and chill for 30 minutes.

Meanwhile make the sauce. Place the onion, pepper, courgette and aubergine in a saucepan along with the bay leaf and chopped tomatoes. Season well, bring to the boil and simmer for 10 minutes until tender. Set aside until ready to serve.

Preheat the grill to a medium-hot setting. Arrange the meatballs on the grill rack and cook for 8-10 minutes, turning frequently until golden all over and cooked through. Drain well.

Reheat the sauce until piping hot, discard the bay leaf and serve the meatballs with the sauce, sprinkled with chopped parsley.

serves 4

each serving is:

Free on Original

Free on Extra Easy

freezer friendly

ready in 40 minutes plus chilling time

4 spring onions, trimmed and finely chopped

450g lean pork, minced

1 tsp dried mixed herbs

salt and freshly ground black pepper

for the sauce

1 small onion, peeled and chopped

1 small yellow pepper, halved, deseeded and finely chopped

1 small courgette, finely chopped

1 baby aubergine, finely chopped

1 bay leaf

400g can chopped tomatoes with garlic

chopped fresh flat-leaf parsley, to garnish

thai
pork curry

serves 4

each serving is:

Free on Original

Free on Extra Easy

freezer friendly

ready in 30-35 minutes

500g lean pork steaks,
all visible fat removed

low calorie cooking spray

2 garlic cloves,
peeled and thinly sliced

1 tbsp very finely
chopped lemon grass

1 red chilli, deseeded
and thinly sliced

6 spring onions,
trimmed and cut into
4cm diagonal pieces

1kg frozen mixed
stir-fry vegetables

200ml chicken stock

1 tbsp Thai 7-spice
seasoning

4 tbsp soy sauce

1 tbsp nam pla
(Thai fish sauce) (optional)

chopped fresh coriander,
to garnish

Stir-frying is a very quick and healthy way of cooking. Using frozen vegetables in this dish makes it extra fast and gives you a delicious all in one meal that loses none of the fresh, tangy Thai flavours of the spices and sauces.

Place the pork steaks between sheets of cling film and, using a wooden mallet or rolling pin, beat until about 5mm thick. Cut the pork into very thin strips.

Spray a large non-stick wok or frying pan with low calorie cooking spray. Place over a high heat and add the pork strips. Stir-fry for 7-8 minutes or until the pork is sealed, cooked through and lightly browned. Add the garlic, lemon grass, red chilli and spring onions and stir-fry for 1-2 minutes.

Stir in the frozen vegetables and cook for 2-3 minutes. Add the stock, Thai 7-spice seasoning, soy sauce and nam pla (if using) and stir and cook for 2-3 minutes or until the vegetables are just tender.

Remove from the heat and serve sprinkled with coriander.

celeriac and pork citrus pot

This is one of those really easy dishes that still tastes delicious. The secret weapon here is lemon juice, which really brings out the great earthy taste of celeriac.

serves 4

each serving is:

Free on Original

Free on Extra Easy

freezer friendly

ready in 50 minutes

Preheat the oven to 190°C/Gas 5. Trim the base and top from the celeriac and peel with a sharp knife. Wash the peeled bulb under cold water. Cut into medium dice and toss in the lemon juice.

Place the pork in a flameproof casserole dish with the leek. Spray with low calorie cooking spray and cook for 5 minutes, stirring continuously.

Add the celeriac and lemon juice to the dish with the stock and tomato purée, stirring well. Cover and cook for 25 minutes in the oven.

Add the green beans to the casserole, season to taste and cook on the hob for a further 5 minutes.

Sprinkle the lemon and orange zest over the top and garnish with the orange segments and parsley.

450g celeriac

zest and juice of 1 lemon

400g lean pork fillet, all visible fat removed, cut into thin strips

1 leek, trimmed and sliced

low calorie cooking spray

300ml vegetable stock

1 level tbsp tomato purée

75g green beans, trimmed and halved

salt and freshly ground black pepper

1 orange, zest grated and flesh cut into segments

chopped fresh flat-leaf parsley, to garnish

pork and mango parcels

The flavours of pork and ripe mango complement each other perfectly in this dish, making it wonderful either as an easy lunch or a light snack.

serves 4

each serving is:

Free on Original

Free on Extra Easy

ready in about 20 minutes

800g lean pork fillets, all visible fat removed, cut into thin slices or strips

2 tbsp light soy sauce

2 tsp garlic granules

2 tsp ground ginger

freshly ground black pepper

low calorie cooking spray

for the parcels

1 iceberg lettuce, separated into 8 large leaves

1 ripe mango, peeled, stoned and finely sliced

110g cherry tomatoes, quartered

a small handful of fresh mint, chopped

Place the pork in a bowl. Mix the soy sauce, garlic granules and ground ginger and season with the pepper. Spoon this mixture over the pork and toss to coat well.

Spray a large, non-stick frying pan with low calorie cooking spray and place over a high heat. Working in batches, cook the pork for 2-3 minutes on each side or until cooked through. Remove from the pan and keep warm.

To serve, line a serving platter with the lettuce leaves. Toss the mango, tomatoes and mint with the pork and divide this mixture between the lettuce leaves. Roll up the leaves and eat immediately.

Duck would also be delicious in this recipe.

index

conversions

We have used metric measurements throughout this book. If you prefer to use imperial measurements, the following lists will help you.

grams/ounces

15g	½oz
25g	1oz
60g	2½oz
75g	3oz
100g	3½oz
110g	4oz (¼lb)
150g	5oz
175g	6oz
200g	7oz
225g	8oz (½lb)
250g	9oz
300g	11oz
350g	12oz (¾lb)
375g	13oz
400g	14oz
450g	16oz (1lb)
500g	18oz (1lb 2oz)
600g	22oz (1lb 6oz)
700g	24oz (1½lb)
800g	28oz (1lb 12oz)
900g	32oz (2lb)
1000g/1kg	36oz (2lb 4oz)
1200g/1.2kg	43oz (2lb 11oz)
3000g/3kg	108oz (6¾lb)

millilitres/fluid ounces/pints

100ml	3½fl oz
125ml	4fl oz
150ml	5fl oz (¼ pint)
200ml	7fl oz
250ml	9fl oz
300ml	11fl oz
350ml	12fl oz
400ml	14fl oz
500ml	18fl oz
600ml	20fl oz (1 pint)
700ml	24fl oz
850ml	30fl oz (1½ pints)

centimetres/inches

5mm	¼ inch
1.5cm	½ inch
2cm	¾ inch
4cm	1½ inches
6cm	2½ inches

Published in 2011 by
Slimming World
Clover Nook Road
Somercotes
Alfreton
Derbyshire
DE55 4RF
UK
www.slimmingworld.com

Editor: Allison Brentnall
Proof reader: Beverley Farnsworth
Designer: Kathryn Briggs

Food stylist: Lorna Brash
Photographer: Karen Thomas
Photography assistant: Laura Urschel
Stylist: Polly Webb-Wilson
Home economists: Sunil Vijayakar, Lorna Brash,
Kathryn Hawkins, Jenny Stacey

Front cover photograph: Pork & herb meatballs with
ratatouille sauce, pg 111

Back cover photographs: top left – ham & egg soufflés,
pg 20; bottom left – seafood stew, pg 40; middle – mustard
& garlic-roasted leg of lamb, pg 76; top right – Thai-style
aromatic chicken stir-fry, pg 52; bottom right – garlicky
chicken casserole, pg 62.